SOUL HEALING:
A GUIDED JOURNAL FOR BLACK WOMEN

SOUL HEALING

A Guided Journal for Black Women

Prompts to Help You Reflect,
Grow, and Embrace Your Power

SHARRON LYNN

ROCKRIDGE
PRESS

To my late mother, Abigail Williams, I carry you with me always.
This one's for you, Ma.

For general information on our other products and services, please contact our Customer Care Department within the United States at (866) 744-2665, or outside the United States at (510) 253-0500.

Paperback ISBN: 978-1-63807-332-1

Manufactured in the United States of America

Interior and Cover Designer: Jennifer Hsu
Art Producer: Megan Baggott
Editor: Crystal Nero
Production Editor: Mia Moran
Production Manager: Jose Olivera

Illustrations © Emma Make/Creative Market. Author photo courtesy of Nuru Dorsey.

10 9 8 7 6 5 4 3 2 1

This journal belongs to:

_____

Contents

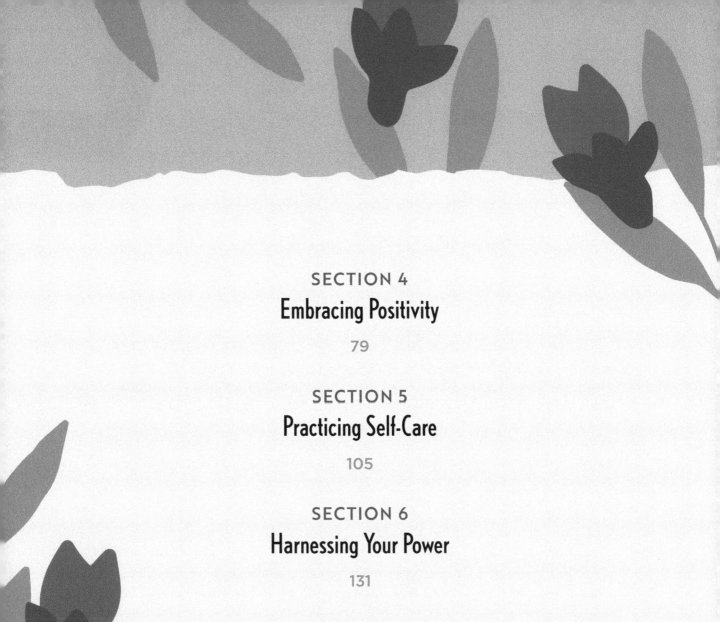

Introduction

Black women are dynamic and resilient beings. We live and love through challenges and triumphs while navigating terrain that is unique to us and only us. The specificity of our experience means we need spaces curated with our individual reality top of mind. This journal is designed to be just that—a safe space for us to reflect, confront, embrace, love, heal, and elevate unapologetically in our Black womanhood.

The narrative of the "strong Black woman" is far too common and restrictive. We're often the foundational pillars in our families, backbones of our communities, and leaders of social movements. Though there is much beauty in our strength, too often the roles we're expected to take on leave us very little room for our own care. We live in a world that continues to perpetuate sexist and racist traumas that we must constantly tackle while finding ways to heal. Frankly, it can be a lot. If we want to thrive in happiness and health, we need to firmly and unapologetically plant ourselves in self-care.

In 2017, I decided to travel to Rishikesh, India, to study yoga for five weeks, and it shaped my ideas around how to love myself in unimaginable ways. Up until that point, I'd struggled profoundly with what it meant to fully love myself. What does self-love truly look like? Feel like? And how do I learn to do it so well that it never leaves me? I took all these questions with me on this cherished journey. My peace is not something I want the outside world to dictate. My peace is not something I will allow the outside world to dictate. I realized my answers were waiting patiently for me in the sacred crevices of my habits and daily practices. My new systems and ways of thinking led to authentic empowerment, and this shift was so profound that I made a pact with myself to share my practices far and wide. Much of what you'll read and work through here has guided me to a discovery of genuine and ever-growing love for my Blackness, my womanhood, and the oh-so-beautiful intersection of them both.

So here we are. This journal isn't designed to replace professional help; it's simply here to be a supplement and source of support. We'll start with some introspection and compassionately work our way toward a more loving state of being using a variety of tools. I encourage you to embrace the journey and lean into any discomfort that may arise. And remember, this isn't time you're *spending on* yourself but rather *investing in* yourself. You have permission to take the incredibly empowering ride of traveling inward, being vulnerable, and rising again and again from a place of clarity and genuine wellness. Our healing is an ongoing, nonlinear journey to unconditional self-love and wholeness. Here's to the collective elevation of all Black women. Let's rise together!

Section 1

REFLECTING ON WHO YOU ARE

In any healing journey, it's important to take some time to sit with who and where we are. Every decision and experience in our lives—good or bad—has been necessary to lead us to this very moment. Gaining clarity by taking an honest look at ourselves is the first leap toward our rise.

"It was when I realized I needed to stop trying to be somebody else and be myself that I actually started to own, accept, and love what I had."

—TRACEE ELLIS ROSS

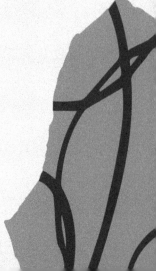

WE ALL CARRY ideas about where we'd like to be at various stages in our lives. If you could craft your life exactly how you wanted it, what would it look like right now?

BEING A BLACK woman comes with a very specific set of challenges. Has there ever been an instance when you felt your Black womanhood was threatening to others? If so, describe what happened and how it made you feel.

OUR MINDSETS ARE extremely powerful in guiding us toward creating the lives we want and deserve. Take some time to explore your default state of mind. Do you generally prepare for the worst or plan for the best? Are you a glass-half-empty or glass-half-full type of thinker? Why do you believe you gravitate to one or the other?

The conversations we have with ourselves can define us in ways we're not always aware of, so it's important to be mindful of our inner dialogue and learn how to interrupt negative thought patterns.

Think of the three most common doubts that arise for you and create three opposing affirmations that you can repeat the next time you catch yourself having these negative thoughts. For example, if your thought tends to be, "I'm not where I should be," your affirmation could be, "I'm exactly where I'm supposed to be, and I'm constantly growing." Consider the new energy you'd like to attract and craft your affirmations to oppose your negative thoughts.

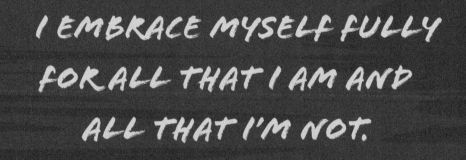

I EMBRACE MYSELF FULLY
FOR ALL THAT I AM AND
ALL THAT I'M NOT.

OUR VALUE SYSTEMS can serve as a compass in our lives while providing insights about what we consider to be important. Do you value community, creativity, compassion, happiness, health, knowledge, love, and trust? With 1 being the most important on your list and 10 being the least important, list 10 personal values that you live by or would like to live by.

WE ALL HAVE qualities that we consider to be strengths. It may be a talent, how we interact with others, or a personality trait that makes us unique. Name your personal superpower. How has it helped you in your life?

THERE ARE CERTAIN stereotypes that are commonly associated with Black women, such as being angry or overly sexual. I can think of a few instances when I felt disappointed by someone's inaccurate perception of me based on my race and gender. In the space that follows, write down three times where you've experienced being stereotyped, followed by the truth of who you are.

Stereotype: _____

    Truth: _____

Stereotype: _____

    Truth: _____

Stereotype: _____

    Truth: _____

Take yourself on a date. This could be a visit to your favorite coffee shop or simply a walk in the park. Wherever you go, be intentional about spending this time with yourself. Unplug from devices for a bit if possible. Take note of your self-talk, sit with what comes up, and pay attention to how it feels to be in your own company. Take some time to write about your experience on a separate sheet of paper and consider the following:

Where did you go?

Did you enjoy the time spent with yourself? Why or why not?

Were you able to fully commit to being with yourself without distractions? Why or why not?

What self-talk did you notice?

LESLIE'S JOURNEY

For the majority of her teenage and adult life, Leslie was stuck in a vicious cycle of comparison. She constantly saw perfection in the lives of others while feeling a sense of lack in her own. After experiencing bouts of depression, Leslie began to see that measuring her life by comparing it to others' lives was diminishing her own sense of value. She started to shift the narrative in her mind by practicing gratitude for her unique gifts and using positive affirmations to quiet negative self-talk. By becoming steadfast in her commitment to love herself and her life more fully, Leslie became more grounded in who and where she is.

IF YOU WERE to ask three random people to share their definitions of success, you'd likely get three very different responses. What do personal and professional success look like to you? Is one more important to you than the other?

WHAT'S ONE GOAL you'd like to reach in the next year in the areas of health, mind, and spirit? Do you want to develop heathier eating habits, take a course to explore an area of interest, or commit a few hours each week to indulging in a hobby that brings you joy? Once you've identified your goals, write about how each of them would enhance your well-being.

NO MATTER HOW great life gets, we all have setbacks. Describe a challenging time that you worked through recently. How did it help you grow or gain new strength?

IN THIS VERY MOMENT,
I AM IN ALIGNMENT
AND EXACTLY WHERE I'M
SUPPOSED TO BE.

I do a bit of goal-mapping two or three times a year to help me identify the steps I need to take in order to achieve a desired change. It's great to have goals, but we increase the likelihood of reaching them when we have a plan. Think of one goal you'd like to accomplish in the next year, either personally or professionally, and five things you can do to get closer to it. Then draw your own diagram like the provided example, placing your goal at the top center and the action steps in the smaller bubbles below.

Goal
Fill my days with more joy.

Action Steps

1 Find a new hobby I truly enjoy.

2 Call a close friend once a week.

3 Create a joy-centered affirmation to use daily.

4 Consume more content that encourages laughter.

5 Visit my favorite spots in nature each week.

LOOKING BACK ON the past 10 years of your life, what are three defining decisions you're proud of yourself for making? Why?

OUR HABITS ARE incredibly powerful tools in shaping our lives. Can you name two personal habits that you need to eliminate? Why are they no longer serving you?

WHEN I THINK of my passion, I think of genuine enjoyment and experiences that allow me to be fully present. What are you most passionate about in your life? What state of mind and spirit are you in while doing it?

TAYLOR'S JOURNEY

Taylor had always had a reputation among her family, friends, and colleagues for being an ambitious high-achiever. She lived what appeared to be a full and privileged life with a thriving career as an attorney. But over time, Taylor began to realize she was terribly unhappy and unfulfilled. She saw that much of her life had been crafted around society's ideas of a successful life—an impressive job title, a luxury car, and social circles with people of the same status. None of this made her happy. Against the wishes of her family and closest friends, Taylor began to move toward working in health and wellness, a career she truly loved. Although she still wanted her loved ones to hold her in high regard, she gathered the courage to push past the judgment of others and is now living a life that brings her genuine joy.

AS BLACK WOMEN, we often feel that we have to stretch ourselves thin for others while neglecting our own needs. But as we progress in our healing journeys, we can cultivate habits that plant us more firmly in our personal power. One habit that has helped me is creating and maintaining boundaries with loved ones when I feel depleted, don't have the capacity, or need to take time for myself. What is a habit that you can create to honor yourself?

THE PEOPLE WE spend the most time with can have a huge impact on our lives. With that in mind, it's important that our closest relationships help us move toward our highest good. Is there a person in your life who encourages and brings out the best in you? Is there someone who focuses on negativity or ignores your boundaries? How so? Briefly describe one person who has a positive impact in your life and one person whose presence is more negative. What feelings do you notice as you write about them?

WHAT WOULD IT look and feel like to you to be fully healed, whole, and complete?

_____

_____

_____

_____

_____

_____

_____

_____

_____

_____

_____

Let's integrate one of the affirmations from this section into a breathing exercise to help us sink a little deeper into self-acceptance. Find a comfortable seated position and allow your spine to be tall. Place your right hand on your heart and your left hand on your belly. Really allow your palms to connect to your body and feel your belly rising and falling as you breathe. On your inhales, think to yourself, "I embrace myself fully for all that I am." On your exhales, think, "I release all that I'm not." Repeat for 10 rounds of slow breath.

"What I know for sure is that speaking your truth is the most powerful tool we all have."

—OPRAH WINFREY

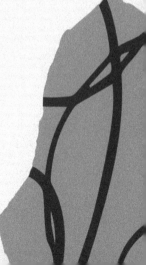

Section 2

WORKING THROUGH COMPLEX FEELINGS

I want you to take a moment to acknowledge your commitment to your healing so far. It's important to celebrate yourself for doing this work because it takes courage to unpack trauma. Now that you've started to identify where you are in your journey, this next section will guide you in tackling your inner challenges. Instead of running away from your pain or trauma, you'll sit down and get to know it intimately so you can see what it's here to teach you, release it, and progress beyond it.

"I realized that I don't have to be perfect. All I have to do is show up and enjoy the messy, imperfect, and beautiful journey of my life."

—KERRY WASHINGTON

THE BEAUTY OF self-awareness is that it empowers us to clarify our feelings, motives, desires, and character without judgment or attachment. Take a moment to check in with yourself and find five short phrases to finish the following sentence. Some examples are "feeling challenged yet hopeful," "uncomfortable in my body," and "proud of my inner work."

In this moment, I'm aware that I am . . .

1. _____

_____

2. _____

_____

3. _____

_____

4. _____

_____

5. _____

_____

IS THERE ANYTHING or anyone that triggers or heightens your anxiety? Consider specific thoughts, people, places, or situations that make it challenging for you to feel at ease. These could be health concerns, sudden life changes, conflict with family or friends, or being in certain social settings. List your triggers and describe the shifts you experience when they're present.

WORRY AND ANXIETY can take up space in our minds and spirits, even when we aren't conscious of them. What are you the most anxious or worried about right now? Do you feel it manifesting in your body anywhere? For example, I tend to experience tightness in my neck when I'm concerned or stressed. Take a moment to explore where you are in your mind and body and write about it. Try not to judge or search for answers or solutions. Simply find language for how you feel and put it on paper.

I once had a ballet teacher who was skilled at calling attention to the places in our bodies holding tension from pent-up emotions. She would gently touch the tense spot and ask us to send breath there. It worked so well that I still practice it. Let's add some of this goodness into a five-minute breathing exercise.

► Make your way into a comfortable seated position.

► Close your eyes and start to breathe in through your nose and out through your mouth.

► Do a mental full-body scan and land on the area that feels the most restricted.

► On every exhale, visualize your breath going to that place. Gently touch the tense spot with both palms, if possible, and imagine the breath leaving your hands and flowing into that spot.

How was this experience for you? Did you feel any shifts in your body?

I EMBRACE THE BEAUTY OF WORKING THROUGH MY PAIN AND TRAUMA FOR THE SAKE OF MY HEALING.

WHILE IT'S IMPORTANT to not let emotions dominate our lives, they do serve an important purpose, so we need to acknowledge them. Emotional shifts can be helpful bits of information that guide us and even help protect us at times. How do you tend to process your emotions when they arise? Do you lean into them or suppress them? Do you have certain beliefs about how you should and shouldn't express emotions? Where do you think those beliefs came from?

DESCRIBE ONE THING that fear is stopping you from doing in any area of your life. What are you most afraid of? List three reasons why it would be worth it to work through the fear and get it done anyway.

A MAJOR PART of our healing work is checking in to ensure we aren't carrying the burden of past experiences. Think of a time in your past when someone caused you emotional pain. If anything comes up that you'd rather not delve into, that's precisely what I recommend you explore. Is this experience still causing you pain? Why do you think that is? How would being fully healed from it enhance your life currently?

It's hard to heal what we don't reveal. Write a letter to a person from your past who caused you emotional pain. Share what happened, how it made you feel, how it has affected you over time, and why it's important to fully release this experience moving forward. If you feel moved to, offer them forgiveness—I highly recommend doing this because the forgiveness is healing for you! If you're willing to take it a step further, mail the letter to the person. You can also have a safe letter-burning ritual or rip the letter to shreds to signify letting go.

What did this process bring up for you? Do you feel a sense of relief? Why or why not?

LISA'S JOURNEY

Most people are drawn to Lisa's vibrant personality. Her colleagues nicknamed her "Sunflower" because she can instantly light up a room with her presence. No one would suspect that she was quietly suffering from unresolved trauma. Lisa never allowed herself to fully confront the hurt and shame she felt from being abused when she was twelve years old. Through therapy, inner reflection, and the support of her friends, Lisa gradually began to heal that old wound. She now has a new appreciation for expressing her pain and facing life's challenges head-on.

VULNERABILITY IS POWERFUL because it allows us to connect to others and live fully in our humanity. How would you define vulnerability? What does it mean to you to be strong? Do you believe you can be strong and vulnerable at the same time? Why or why not? Has your upbringing or any experience from your past shaped your views on this?

WHILE TRYING TO be "strong," we sometimes hold a lot in. It's important to know that we're allowed to be sad, cry, and fully feel every drop of pain we experience. The infamous Black woman survival approach of being tough and sucking it up doesn't serve us. I love and embrace a good, purging cry. When was the last time you felt sad, and why? Did this feeling reveal anything new to you? How do you feel after you cry?

WHEN I THINK of confidence, I think of firmness, trust, and conviction in how I go about life. Fill in the blanks with three words that come to mind for you:

When I think of confidence, I think of _____ *,*

_____ *, and* _____ *.*

NEXT, NAME ONE thing that enhances your self-confidence and one that diminishes it. As a suggestion, consider a good or bad habit or a specific thought.

_____

_____

_____

_____

_____

_____

_____

_____

_____

_____

I find it helpful to keep quotes and inspiring visuals in places where I can see them daily. Take five sticky notes, index cards, or small pieces of paper and, on each one, write an affirmation to keep you encouraged during your healing journey. Feel free to use an affirmation from this section and write the same one on all five. Think about the five personal spaces you're in the most—your office, bedroom, kitchen, bathroom, or car—and place an affirmation in a visible place in each of them.

I AM ACTIVELY TRANSFORMING AND GROWING IN BODY, MIND, AND SPIRIT.

SOMETHING THAT DRIVES me on my life journey is knowing how I can help other people by sharing my challenges. When I share my story, it helps others feel less alone and often encourages them to overcome their own challenges. Can you think of a time when a challenge of yours served someone else? If so, describe how. If not, think of one way you could use one of your challenges to help someone else and jot down how you envision yourself doing that.

AS BLACK WOMEN, we're often expected to carry the weight of the world. I believe it's safe to say it's time to break free of this way of thinking and being. What's one area of your life where you need help? Are you okay with asking for help? Why or why not?

IMPOSTER SYNDROME OFTEN makes us believe false ideas about ourselves and keeps negative thoughts on a loop. It's helpful to combat these thoughts with affirmations that highlight your strengths. Explore a time when you felt you weren't good enough or deserving of an accomplishment. What are three kind things you can say about yourself right now to oppose those negative thoughts? For example, "I love that I'm kind and people feel comfortable opening up to me."

ASHLEY'S JOURNEY

Ashley's battle with imposter syndrome was crippling. She'd talk herself out of just about any positive change, opportunity, and even dates with potential life partners because she struggled profoundly with self-worth and believed that she didn't deserve great things. Ashley knew that unless she changed her mindset, she'd never fulfill her potential or enjoy fresh, empowering, and exciting life experiences. To overcome her negative self-talk, she surrounded herself with people who affirmed the best in her, and she created uplifting mantras to repeat throughout the day. At the end of each day, she listed the ways she made herself proud. The following year, Ashley landed an executive position in her field and met the man who would later become her fiancé, both just months apart. Her mindset adjustment attracted wonderful shifts that reflect the positive ways she now perceives herself.

OF ALL THE women you know, personally or not, who stands out to you as radiating a high level of self-esteem? What about them tells you this? Do you see any of these characteristics in your current or future self?

_____

_____

_____

_____

_____

_____

_____

_____

_____

_____

_____

_____

ARE THERE ANY situations from your past or present that you feel shame or guilt about? Describe what happened as well as how you would've liked to see the situation play out. Next, explore one way that experience actually helped your growth and development.

IF YOU COULD go back and share one piece of advice with your younger self, what would it be? Approach this as a brief love letter to the younger you, offering encouragement and even forgiveness if needed.

Our body language can play a huge role in shaping our confidence. Unless you're dealing with physical restrictions, a slouching posture can signal laziness and low self-esteem to your mind and to people you interact with. Take a moment to make your way into the following "power pose." (Confession: I once did this in a restroom stall before a meeting, and it helped ease my nerves and lift my confidence tremendously!)

- ▸ Stand with your feet a little wider than your hips and plant them firmly.

- ▸ Make a fist with your hands and place them on your waist.

- ▸ Lift your chin slightly with a proud and lifted chest and spine.

- ▸ Hold for five rounds of breath while repeating, "I am grounded in unshakable confidence."

How was this experience for you? Did you feel any mental or physical shifts?

"When you understand your inner self—your passions, motivations, moral code, and vulnerabilities, you don't have to blow in the wind of someone else's expectations; you can stand firm in your own truth."

—JANET AUTHERINE

Section 3

TREATING YOURSELF WITH COMPASSION

Compassion is one of the best gifts we can give ourselves. It's interesting how we are sometimes kinder, gentler, and more encouraging to others than we are to ourselves—I've been guilty of it too! The great news is that we can alter this narrative with our practices. Here you'll find tools to help you actively work on your relationship with self-compassion and self-respect.

"What actually sustains us, what is fundamentally beautiful, is compassion–for yourself and for those around you. That kind of beauty inflames the heart and enchants the soul."

—LUPITA NYONG'O

OUR MORNING ROUTINES are vital in helping us set the tone for the day. It's not just about what we do in the mornings but also how we think. What's your general default state of mind in the mornings? Do you have kind thoughts about yourself? What are two complimentary phrases you could say to yourself while preparing for your day?

WHAT'S YOUR FAVORITE physical quality about yourself? Describe how it makes you feel and what you love most about it.

THINK OF THE most stressful situation in your life right now. If your closest friend or family member were facing the same challenge, what advice would you offer them?

Our bodies are beautiful instruments of all shapes and sizes that carry us through life. They truly do a lot for us! Take some time to indulge in some well-deserved body appreciation. While going for a 10-minute walk in nature, have a sincere chat with your body and thank it for all it is and all it does. Remember to include everything from your hair down to your toes. You can even write a letter to it to take it a step further.

I AM BEAUTIFUL IN EVERY WAY, EVERY DAY.

WE SHOW UP to some days stronger than others. That's just part of life, and it's important that we allow ourselves grace on the more challenging days. On those harder days, how do you talk to yourself? Do you tend to treat yourself kindly, or are you harsher than necessary? What would you like to do differently when you process days like this?

WHEN WE'RE GENTLE with ourselves, we can embrace the power of self-respect. With this also comes the beauty of riding the inevitable waves of life with less stress. What are three ways you can be gentler with yourself?

I HAVEN'T ALWAYS thought this way, but I've learned to celebrate myself when-ever possible. "Make yourself proud" is a simple mantra that I keep posted in any space I spend a lot of time in. Take a moment to celebrate yourself right now. Describe two ways you've made yourself proud in your life—remember, no win is too small to mention!

Self-compassion is a wonderful antidote to our inner critic. The more we practice it, the more we experience the magic of truly loving ourselves. Try the following exercise to strengthen your compassionate voice.

1. Gently close your eyes or look at a point on the ground directly in front of you.

2. Make sure you're in a state of calmness and then think of a situation that's currently challenging you.

3. Notice the feeling in your body and allow it to be there without judgment or resistance.

4. Now repeat the following to yourself five times:

    This is a challenging moment.

    Challenges are part of my life journey.

    I give myself the compassion I need to work through it.

How was this experience for you? Were you able to shift your energy regarding the challenging circumstance?

TARA'S JOURNEY

Tara is a striking woman with alluring eyes, a bright smile, and beautiful dark brown skin. But she often felt her complexion was less of a gift and more of a curse. When Tara was 17, a modeling agency rejected her, rudely saying that it was because she was "darker than they needed" at the time. Tara was crushed and carried many image insecurities over the years, assuming that if something didn't work out, it was because of her skin color. But at 29, she was finally ready to stop letting society's colorism issues discourage her and to start celebrating everything about herself. She intentionally submerged herself in books and media that uplifted Black women of all shades, complimented herself often, and created an initiative to help teenage Black girls tackle image issues. Now 39, Tara lives her life with a profoundly grounded sense of love and respect for herself.

A POSITIVE ATTRIBUTE is a strength, skill, or character trait that's helpful to us and others. Let's shine a light on yours. What would you say are your five best attributes? Are you kind, intelligent, patient, authentic, fun, honest? What are some other attributes that you'd like to cultivate as you grow?

THINK OF THE kindest person you know or have ever met. What did they do to exude such kindness? Is this something you'd do for yourself? Why or why not?

WHAT WOULD IT look like to go through a full day loving yourself unconditionally? In other words, from the time you wake up to the time you return to sleep, what sort of things would you do throughout the day to show up for yourself in the most loving way possible?

Treat yourself! There's nothing like a kind gesture to fill your tank and put a smile on your own face. Do something nice for yourself, such as picking up a bouquet of your favorite flowers, making your favorite meal, or performing a self-massage after a warm shower. Whatever you do, allow it to come from a place of genuine kindness.

WE ARE ALL imperfect beings—or, as a T-shirt of mine reads, "perfectly imperfect." I believe life would be pretty boring and uneventful if we weren't, because imperfections give us something to work toward. For me, embracing my imperfections means accepting that I'll always have them, as well as creating a loving, healthy relationship with them that encourages my expansion and evolution. Can you name two things about yourself that you consider imperfections? What would it look like to make peace with them but also use them to help you grow?

UNREALISTIC EXPECTATIONS CAN imprison our minds and spirits for no good reason. When we have them, we bind ourselves to an idea or way of being that isn't aligned with our path. Releasing these expectations can be incredibly liberating. Do you have any unrealistic expectations of yourself or your life's trajectory? What would it look like to let go of them?

TRYING TO LIVE up to the standards or expectations of others can be quite a burden. A big part of loving ourselves is ensuring we're not bending too much to please others. Is there someone close to you who has an unrealistic expectation of you? If so, how has this affected you? How could you encourage yourself to fully release these expectations?

DEON'S JOURNEY

Deon is a wife and mother of three who felt enormously guilty about carving out time for herself. Outside of work, she and her husband shared the responsibility of getting the kids to their evening extracurricular activities, but making dinner and most of the household cleaning fell almost solely on Deon. "I can't afford to take time away from my family," she'd think, or, "If I step away, the house would fall apart." In reality, her lack of care for herself caused her to nearly fall apart. Deon's anxiety increased, she stopped working out often, and she eventually reached a breaking point. Then she decided to ask her husband for help—and he was incredibly supportive. They arranged for their parents to help out two evenings per week, allowing Deon time to invest in herself more often. She now enjoys nonnegotiable, guilt-free time every week to nurture herself.

I AM PLANTED FIRMLY
IN MY OWN LOVE, RESPECT,
AND COMPASSION.

WHEN I THINK of my value, I think of my strengths and what I have to offer the world around me. For example, I have gained a great deal of yoga knowledge that I'm able to share with family, friends, and colleagues when they need it. What's one valuable thing about you that has contributed to your world? Explain how.

ARE THERE ANY people or situations that you feel are barriers to your self-care? Describe how they're hindering you from getting what you need. How could you kindly handle the person or situation to minimize this moving forward?

WHEN WE PUT things into our own words, it helps us gain clarity and power because we're then able to define where we stand. Create your own definitions of self-love, self-respect, and self-confidence. Play with the language until the definitions completely embody your understanding of each one. There are no wrong answers, and they may even change in the future as you continue to evolve.

I'm a true believer in the healing power of music and dance, and research shows that dancing can improve our mental health. I'm no stranger to a solo dance party, and I often have days where I dance to my favorite tunes for a mood boost. It's the best! Find one song that inspires you to celebrate yourself fully, crank up the volume if you can, and don't stop dancing until the song ends. Some of my favorites are "Q.U.E.E.N." by Janelle Monáe featuring Erykah Badu, "Feeling Good" by Nina Simone, "Private Party" by India.Arie, and "Golden" by Jill Scott. Have a blast with this one and repeat whenever you need a pick-me-up.

"Don't wait around for other people to be happy for you. Any happiness you get you've got to make yourself."

—ALICE WALKER

Section 4

EMBRACING POSITIVITY

The power we have to shape our mindset is beyond measure. When we learn to let a positive state of mind take the lead, we can truly feel unstoppable. It helps us trust that life is rigged in our favor, and we become precisely what we want to attract into our lives. This section is designed to help you cultivate that sweet space and gently guide you back when you stray from it. It's such a delightful place to call home—let's dive on in.

"Freeing yourself was one thing, claiming ownership of that freed self was another."

—TONI MORRISON

GRATITUDE WORKS WONDERS in our lives. When we find the beauty in who we are and what we have, we attract more goodness and more things to be grateful for. Indulge in what's beautiful in your life and list five things you're grateful for at this very moment and why.

LIMITING BELIEFS ARE such little tricksters. They negatively impact our lives and stop us from living up to our full potential. "Things just don't work out for me," and, "I'm not good enough," are both examples of limiting beliefs. In the spirit of reclaiming your power, bring your limiting beliefs to light and flip them on their heads. What are two limiting beliefs you suspect you may have? Replace them with empowering beliefs. For example, "I'm not good enough," can be changed to, "I am fully equipped for greatness."

I KNEW PERSONAL growth was happening when I realized my setbacks were like slingshots pulling me back to propel me forward. They're unavoidable, but the real magic lies in how they shape us. What's one setback you had in the past year? Were you kind to yourself when working through it? Did it strengthen you in any way? Explore ways in which the experience was necessary to shape the current or future you.

Practice being your own bestie and life coach. Draw a line down the center of a sheet of paper, creating two columns. On the left side, make a list of the criticisms you have of yourself most often. For each criticism, write a statement of encouragement in the right column. Think of advice you'd say to a friend or loved one if they needed it. In this case, the loved one is you.

What was this experience like for you? Did you notice any shifts in yourself as you were writing the encouraging statements?

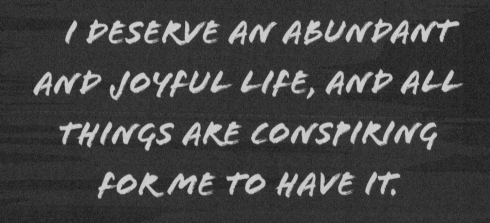

I DESERVE AN ABUNDANT AND JOYFUL LIFE, AND ALL THINGS ARE CONSPIRING FOR ME TO HAVE IT.

ENERGY IS CONTAGIOUS. One valuable lesson I've learned is to pay attention to how I feel when I leave a person. I've felt cloudy leaving certain people and cheerful leaving others. Take a good look at the people you have in your life. Is there anyone who depletes you or brings you toxic energy? How so? Whom do you feel your best around, and what about them makes you feel this way?

THE WAY WE view ourselves is often influenced by society's perceptions of Black women. This can show up in how we perceive the beauty of our hair, body type, and skin tone. Thinking positively about ourselves shapes how we embrace the beautiful bodies we were born in. In what ways do you feel the power of positive thinking can contribute to your physical well-being?

I BELIEVE WE all have a personal hall of fame for our life moments that make us even the slightest bit proud. Make a list of what you'd consider to be your top five accomplishments of all time. Describe how you feel about yourself when you think of them, including words like *strong*, *competent*, *creative*, *generous*, and *hard-working* in your description. What do you think these achievements say about you as a person?

I completely adore personalized love notes. I've even been known to write them to myself in the gift message box when ordering online. It's the absolute best. I want you to create your own love notes to have when you need them.

1. Find a jar or other small empty container around your home, preferably with a lid.

2. Take a few sheets of paper and cut them up into 25 small pieces.

3. Write one kind thing about yourself on each paper. An example might be, "I am beautiful inside and out."

4. Fold them up individually and place them in the container.

5. Feel free to decorate your love-note holder to your liking to give it some pizzazz.

Whenever you're having a rainy day or just need a little extra love, reach in and pull out one of your notes.

SHAWNA'S JOURNEY

Shawna takes pride in the friendships she's maintained since childhood. One summer, after spending a lot of time with two of her long-time friends, Shawna began to notice a shift in her energy. Her thought patterns became more negative, and she was comparing herself to others more often. Shawna realized this mental shift was directly correlated to the time she was spending with her friends, who liked to engage in gossip and negative chat. For the sake of self-preservation, she knew she had to pull back. She gradually spent less time with them, making space to get to know colleagues and other people in her life. Her newer connections brought the positivity she needed back into her world. Shawna now understands the importance of being selective about the company she keeps because it has the power to alter how she shows up in the world.

SOME VICTORIES IN life can taste a little sweeter than others, simply because of what they require of us. They give us the chance to find our inner strength. What's one big obstacle you were able to overcome in the past? Describe your process of coming to terms with the challenge and how you were able to conquer it.

OUR HABITS ARE incredibly powerful tools, especially when we're working toward personal growth. When we do something consistently, it becomes a part of our behavior, and it can even build our character. What are three positive habits you'd like to add to your daily routine? In what ways do you feel they'll improve your quality of life?

DESCRIBE WHAT A winning day looks like to you. From beginning to end, what sorts of things would have to happen in order for you to feel as though you've won the day? How would you celebrate yourself for it?

There aren't many things that can shift my mood and energy the way music can. It's truly powerful. Create a playlist of at least 10 of your favorite feel-good songs and listen to it when you want to return to a positive state of mind or need a pick-me-up.

Did you feel anything, such as a sense of joy or pleasure, while putting the list together? Why or why not?

I ONCE WORKED with a life coach who constantly reminded me to "be like water." This mantra has helped me remain flexible and keep an open mind while working toward my life and career goals. Imagine the ability water has to flow down a river and over rocks, and shape itself around anything placed in it. How could your life be enhanced by flowing like water and living with an open mind instead of being rigid and unchanging?

THOUGH WE SHOULD strive to keep a positive mindset, we shouldn't reject difficult emotions in an effort to remain "happy." Challenges are necessary, and it's important to deal with them honestly and without toxic positivity. Create two affirmations to help you navigate tough moments in a loving but positive way. For example, "I will work through this tough moment with grace. I welcome everything that it's here to teach me."

THERE IS INCREDIBLE power in language and our ability to speak life and love into ourselves. What are five self-empowering words you'd use to describe yourself? Some examples are *radiant*, *kind*, *intelligent*, and *resilient*. Once you have them, use them to write a loving paragraph about yourself.

LIZ'S JOURNEY

There should be an image of Liz in the dictionary next to the word *ambitious*. Her work ethic is fierce and consistent at a level you don't often see. But deep down, Liz struggled with a sense of scarcity. The things she accomplished never seemed to satisfy her. In fact, each goal she reached created more anxiety and a stronger desire for more. A mentor of hers noticed this unhealthy pattern and introduced the idea of keeping a gratitude journal. Liz took this advice and started a morning practice of jotting down five things she was grateful for each day. What she experienced was simply transformative, and she describes it as "a boundless sense of fullness and a deep level of contentment." Not only did she start to feel good, but opportunities also flowed to her without the excessive grind she was used to. Her gratitude practice was truly life-changing.

I AM GRATEFUL FOR
MY PAST, MY PRESENT,
AND ALL THE GOODNESS
MANIFESTING FOR
MY FUTURE.

NAME THREE THINGS that went well today without considering how small or insignificant they may be. It if went well, write it down. It's all deserving of recognition.

MANY OF US struggle to find motivation at times, myself included. What are your usual thought patterns when you're feeling the least motivated? Can you make any mindset adjustments to help you get the spark you need to move forward?

THINK OF YOURSELF as a living field of energy that can be altered by your mental state. The beauty of developing a more positive, uplifting mindset is that others can feel it and benefit from it, and we become magnets for many of the same magical vibes. In what ways can your positive energy and mindset enhance the lives of others? How do you think you can embody that energy more often?

Physical exercise is a great way to increase motivation. Set your timer for 10 minutes and engage in some sort of physical activity for that time. It could be a walk or jog around the block, walking up and down the stairs in your home, or even a vigorous dance session. When you're done, jump right into a task you want to complete. Did you feel a burst of energy going from the physical activity to the task?

"As Black women, we're always given
these seemingly devastating experiences-
experiences that could absolutely break us.
But what the caterpillar calls the end of the world,
the master calls the butterfly. What we do as
Black women is take the worst situations
and create from that point."

—VIOLA DAVIS

Section 5

PRACTICING SELF-CARE

Creating a consistent self-care practice is invaluable. It helps you cultivate a healthy relationship with yourself and opens you up to better serve others. Here you'll explore where you currently are in your self-care practice as well as ways to strengthen it. May you walk confidently knowing that you deserve to invest time and energy into your nonnegotiable self-care.

"Caring for myself is not self-indulgence,
it is self-preservation, and
that is an act of political warfare."

—AUDRE LORDE

IT'S LOVELY TO feel cared for, whether that care comes from ourselves or others. Think of a moment from your past when you were truly cared for, and in as much detail as possible, describe how it made you feel. Did you find yourself showing up in the world differently in any capacity? Did you feel more confident or assured? Why or why not? How can you regularly care for yourself in that way?

RIDING THE WAVES of life can be depleting, especially when we're required to navigate microaggressions, inequities, personal safety, and caring for ourselves and loved ones. It's important to have ways to recharge when we notice our tanks running low. What do you currently do when you feel you need to recharge? If you could have it exactly the way you wanted it, how would you spend a full day nurturing yourself?

I'M A FIRM believer in intentional joy as a practice of self-care. At least once a month, I make sure to enjoy a group chat with my girlfriends. We talk about anything and everything and often laugh until our stomachs hurt. It's the most replenishing time that I truly look forward to. What experiences bring you the most joy, and how can you create space for more of them in your life?

Sometimes self-care looks like trying something new! The feeling of adventure and novelty can bring out a sweet, childlike energy in us that can be exciting and liberating. Treat yourself to a new experience of your choice. Maybe you finally go to that place in your hometown that you've always wanted to visit. Or you head to a new spot in nature to explore, or pack up and visit a destination nearby for a day or two. Whatever you decide, the focus is to hold space for yourself and allow the newness to fill you up.

What did this experience do for you? Did you feel cared for and as if you were creating space for yourself to feel joy? Why or why not?

IT'S COMMON TO struggle with feelings of guilt when we need to carve out time for ourselves. We often bend toward being the nurturers and caretakers of others, even at the expense of our own needs. Explore your thoughts about taking time for your self-care. Do you ever have mindset blocks stopping you from indulging in your own nurturing? If so, how do you work through them?

WHAT'S ONE THING you wish you had more time for and why? Write down three ways you can strategically work toward finding the time to make this wish come true.

ONE OF THE most valuable lessons I've learned and relearned is the power of boundaries. Saying "no" or "not now" can be challenging, but the price we pay for not standing firm in our boundaries can cause us spiritual and mental harm. How do you feel about boundaries? Have you established them for yourself? Take some time to write out what they are as well as the boundaries you'd like to implement moving forward.

Indulge in a warm, relaxing bath with the help of some goodies. Feel free to grab a flower and add petals to your water, burn a candle, bring in a glass of your favorite beverage, and place a book on the side to enjoy. You can even play soothing tunes in the background. If there's anyone else in your household, be sure to request that they not interrupt you during this precious time of self-care.

ERICA'S JOURNEY

Erica is a loving single mother of two teenage boys who works a full-time job. She'd often tell herself that the time she spent with the boys on the weekends was exactly what she needed to reset each week. But even though she loved time with her kids, a health scare caused her to reevaluate her self-care practices. At one doctor's visit, Erica learned that she'd suffered a mild heart attack as a result of chronic stress. All of her time and energy were wrapped up in work and the duties of motherhood, leaving nothing for herself. She slowly started carving out time on the weekends to meet up with girlfriends and treat herself to alone time away from home, allowing the boys to be a little more independent. Erica's stress levels decreased drastically, and she now enjoys the benefits of caring for herself more intentionally.

MY WANTS AND NEEDS
ARE AS IMPORTANT AS
ANYONE ELSE'S.

MORNING ROUTINES ARE imperative because they play a huge role in setting the tone for the day. A few morning practices that work for me are breathing exercises, meditation, journaling, and making a healthy smoothie. If I skip any of them, there's a noticeable difference in how grounded I feel that day. Do you currently have a morning routine? What are three practices you could add to it to help set you up for a solid day?

ON A DAY when you're at your absolute busiest, how can you find 10 minutes for yourself? What could you do to re-center yourself in that time?

DISCIPLINE IS A form of self-care. When we love ourselves enough to hold ourselves accountable time and time again, we benefit greatly. What is your relationship with discipline? Where in your life would you like to implement more discipline?

As we navigate our days, it's important to be mindful of not living in the past or future. Take three minutes to enjoy this present moment meditation to reset and bring your focus back to the now.

Wherever you are, standing or sitting, find stillness and lower your gaze. As you breathe deeply, check in with all five senses. What do you currently see, smell, feel, taste, and hear? Simply acknowledge what's there.

Anytime you feel as if you've strayed away from the present moment, dive into this meditative exercise to return to it.

WHAT WOULD IT look like for you stay clear of distractions from your self-care? Are there conversations you'd need to have to set boundaries with loved ones? Would devices have to be powered down? Brainstorm a game plan for what exactly would need to happen in order for you to fully engage in quality time caring for yourself.

WHEN DO YOU feel you're the best version of yourself? What kinds of things are you doing? Are you with others or alone at that time? What is your mindset like? Explore this in as much detail as possible.

IN THE SPIRIT of working to maintain a truly fulfilling life, what's one thing you could do once a week, starting right now, that your future self will love you for in a year? What would it take for you to commit to getting it done every week? It could be something like a yoga session, a rejuvenating soak in the tub, spending an hour reading, or going for a walk in nature.

I DESERVE THE TIME AND ENERGY IT TAKES TO KEEP MY TANK FULL.

DEBRA'S JOURNEY

It's truly a gift to have someone you can call when you need an ear, and Debra is that go-to person for her family and friends. She values knowing her loved ones can count on her when they need her, and she's deeply respected for her capacity to love. But Debra was always so open and available to everyone else that she neglected to pay attention to her own needs. After suffering a depressive episode, she knew she had to create boundaries around being accessible to others, so she openly shared her mental health struggles with loved ones and outlined the days and times that she would be unreachable. Debra now stands firmly in her boundaries and commitment to caring for her mind, body, and spirit.

A KEY TO emotional health is staying clear of the joy killer known as comparison. We are each unique and special in our way, and there's room for us all to exist in our greatness. And besides, there's much less traffic when you're in your own lane. In what ways do you hold space for yourself when comparison creeps in? What are your unique characteristics, both physically and personally?

AS CHALLENGING AS it can be, finding the courage to step up and speak out when necessary is one way we can care for ourselves. Black women often face unique challenges in the workforce and society at large, and it's important to find language for the difficulties we face. Is there any area of your life in which you need to advocate for yourself? Consider both your work and personal life and start by writing out what needs to be communicated.

I want

I need

I expect

I require

IT'S IMPORTANT TO know when to take a breath, slow down, and come back to the present moment. What helps you slow down and feel more present? How could you get into the habit of doing this more often?

Ensuring we get good-quality rest is one amazing way to care for ourselves. There are countless studies that show how rest affects our bodies and minds and helps manage our stress levels. Before going to bed tonight, take five minutes to breathe deeply and do a little stretching to prepare for a night of deep rest. Gently stretch your neck by tilting your head from side to side; then let your upper body fold over bent knees while seated to release your lower spine. Start to encourage your mind to quiet down as you continue to breathe. Once five minutes are up, make your way into your preferred resting position and continue breathing deeply until you drift into slumber.

"Women have been trained in our culture and society to ask for what we want instead of taking what we want. We've been really indoctrinated with this culture of permission. I think it's true for women, and I think it's true for people of color. It's historic, and it's unfortunate and has somehow become part of our DNA. But that time has passed."

—AVA DUVERNAY

Section 6

HARNESSING YOUR POWER

What a wonderful ride we've been on so far! I am honored that you've allowed me to be on this journey with you, and I commend you for doing this healing work. You are worthy and powerful beyond measure, my friend. Welcome to this newer and ever-expanding version of yourself. Spread your wings, allow the tools in this section to help you embrace that power, and continue to soar!

"Don't settle for average. Bring your best
to the moment. Then, whether it fails or succeeds,
at least you know you gave all you had. We need
to live the best that's in us."

—ANGELA BASSETT

HEALING WORK IS life-altering. It empowers us to honor the seasons of life, gain wisdom and growth from our challenges, and reclaim our narratives. I hope you are emboldened as the author of your story. When you think of every nook and cranny of yourself mentally, spiritually, and professionally, what does happiness look like to you? What would need to be in place for you to feel genuinely fulfilled?

LET'S REVEL IN the amazingness of our Black womanhood for a moment. History has shown us how resilient, inventive, bold, and bright we are. I simply adore us! What do you love most about being a Black woman, and why?

THE WORK YOU'VE done in this journal has given you a tool belt of exercises, affirmations, and mindsets to use whenever you need them. One thing that's certain is that life will ebb and flow. You'll have great days and not-so-great days. Which tools will you use when the going gets tough?

There are things that are working for us on this life journey and things that aren't. In this exercise that was introduced to me by my acting and career coach Christine Horn, you'll create lists that'll serve as reminders of these things. Grab two index cards or sheets of paper of any size and label one "Keep Doing List" or "KDL" and the other "Quit Doing List" or "QDL." Next, create lists of all the habits, actions, and thoughts that are either helping or hurting your progress. Put your lists in a place where you can see them daily, such as your bathroom mirror or refrigerator.

MY LOVE FOR MYSELF
KEEPS ME GROUNDED
IN MY POWER AND ROOTED
IN MY TRUTH.

LIVING INTENTIONALLY IS a wonderful way to approach our days. We can achieve this by actively living in alignment with our values, which is one of the highest forms of self-love in my opinion. What does intentional living mean to you? What are three ways you could implement this way of being into your lifestyle?

LOOKING AT YOUR journey so far as a woman and person of color, explore what you've learned about your strengths and capacity to endure. Take a moment to think of these invaluable lessons and use them to finish the following sentences.

I've learned that I'm capable of _____

_____

_____

_____

_____

_____

I've grown to see strengths in myself, such as _____

_____

_____

_____

_____

_____

_____

RISING IN OUR power also involves pursuing the things that bring us the most fulfillment and joy. Think of one thing you've always wanted to do in your professional life. What is it? What's been stopping you? More importantly, what steps will you actively take to make it happen moving forward?

See it, believe it, achieve it. This simple phrase is packed with so much truth. Take some time to lend yourself to the power of visualization. Close your eyes and imagine yourself standing on top of a mountain overlooking the most gorgeous view you've ever seen. As you stand there, visualize yourself feeling grounded, confident, and open to all the greatness life has in store for you. You can even repeat that as a mantra by saying, "I am grounded, confident, and open to all the greatness life has in store for me." Stay there and hold your visualization for 10 rounds of deep breath.

What did you feel while doing this exercise? Was it challenging or easy to keep the visual? Did you feel differently after? If so, describe how you felt.

JADE'S JOURNEY

Jade's story is a great example of what it means to persevere. After four kids and 16 years of marriage, life as she knew it changed drastically in a matter of months. When she learned the devastating truth of her husband's infidelity, Jade filed for divorce and found herself in a paralyzing state of heartbreak. With the help of supportive family members, therapy, and a fierce commitment to heal, Jade began to regain her strength and prepare for a new season of life. Not only did she bounce back, she discovered pieces of herself that had been long suppressed in an effort to fit the expectations of her spouse. She continues to thrive with a deep appreciation for the challenges she endured because they led her to a more empowered version of herself.

THE CAPACITY TO recover from difficulty has always been necessary for us to exist in our marginalized bodies. To be resilient is to have the ability to use your strengths, skills, and resources to handle setbacks. What is your relationship with resilience, and how can you strengthen it?

I ENCOURAGE YOU to continue doing the work it takes to truly trust that you deserve an amazing and abundant life. That's when you'll start to attract that life and true manifestation will begin. When you think of your deepest desires, do you feel any resistance toward them? Do you absolutely believe you can have these things? Explore what it will take to stay in a mental space of "I deserve an amazing and abundant life."

I TRULY CAN'T stress enough the importance of healthy friendships. They have the power to help in personal development, provide support, reduce stress, and decrease feelings of isolation and loneliness. That being said, it's a good idea to stay open to cultivating new bonds when needed. Is there a person who shares your values with whom you'd like to build a relationship? What are some ways you can be intentional about building that with them or any new lovely human with whom you may cross paths?

Getting yourself into a healthy and uplifting state of mind in the mornings is an amazing practice that can keep you aligned with your purpose and power. I have a few motivational speakers in rotation that I listen to first thing in the morning, and it's truly been transformative. Brainstorm a list of mindset goodies you can depend on when your alarm goes off in the mornings. Feel free to add video links to motivational speeches, quotes, or songs that get you in your zone. For the next two weeks, try picking something off the list every day after you wake up and take note of any changes in your mindset.

TO FULLY RISE in your power and become the highest version of yourself, it's important to do what's necessary to make *yourself* a priority. Let's be honest, it's hard to be your best when you're at the end of the line for nourishment. Being as specific as possible, describe how you can prioritize yourself in your daily life, specifically when dealing with any personal, societal, or professional obstacles.

WHAT WOULD YOU do in life if you knew you couldn't fail? Another way to think of it is this: If you woke up to your dream life tomorrow, how would it look?

INSPIRATION IS A powerful tool. It keeps us striving for our greatness when we feel we don't have it in us to take that extra step. Create a list of your top five inspirations. Think of people, books, films, or any experiences you may have had in your life.

1. _____

_____

2. _____

_____

3. _____

_____

4. _____

_____

5. _____

_____

NASHA'S JOURNEY

Nasha had always dreamed of a career as a university professor in education. She'd constantly visualize herself on campus, in administrative meetings, and giving lectures. After she finished her bachelor's degree, the plan was to teach at a high school and move on to higher education in a couple of years. As life would have it, 12 years passed before Nasha made it back to school. But she realized that, unless she truly gave her dream a shot, she'd never feel truly fulfilled, so she began to peel back the layers of fear to work toward writing the story she'd always envisioned for herself. She cracked down, went to graduate school, and eventually received her PhD in education. It was much later in life than expected, but Nasha made her dream of becoming a professor a living reality.

I AM UNIQUE AND SPECIAL IN MY OWN WAY, AND I'M READY TO LIVE AND THRIVE IN THAT KNOWING.

I'VE FOUND INCREDIBLE power in realizing life has its seasons. Each season or chapter of your life will look different, but they're all integral parts of your story. If you had to give this current season of your life a name, what would it be, and why? What would you like the name of the next chapter to be?

BY MOVING TOWARD a more healed version of ourselves, we gain even more knowledge and wisdom about the human experience. It's important to use these gifts to pour into others who may need them, the best way we can. As you continue to thrive and live in your power, in what ways do you want to inspire and give to those in your world?

YOU'VE BEEN DOING the rewarding work of becoming more self-aware, moving out of your comfort zone, developing your strengths, and boosting your confidence. We're often able to gain a more solid understanding of ourselves when we talk it out or write it down. How would you describe to a loved one the ways in which you're currently growing and changing?

Reward yourself for doing this work, friend. You deserve it! Indulge in your favorite meal, pour your favorite beverage, turn on your favorite film, or blast your favorite tunes. You could even go all out and get dressed up. It's a celebration of your incredible healing journey and all the greatness you're manifesting in your life.

"My mission in life is not merely to survive, but to thrive; and to do so with some passion, some compassion, some humor, and some style."

—MAYA ANGELOU

Resources

BOOKS

Brown, Brené. *Daring Greatly: How the Courage to Be Vulnerable Transforms the Way We Live, Love, Parent, and Lead*. New York: Avery, 2012.

Clear, James. *Atomic Habits: An Easy & Proven Way to Build Guild Habits & Break Bad Ones*. New York: Avery, 2018.

Coelho, Paulo. The Alchemist. New York: HarperOne, 1993.

Delia, Lalah. *Vibrate Higher Daily: Live Your Power*. New York: HarperOne, 2019.

Obama, Michelle. *Becoming*. New York: Crown, 2018.

Rhimes, Shonda. *Year of Yes: How to Dance It Out, Stand in the Sun and Be Your Own Person*. New York: Simon & Schuster, 2015.

Ruiz, Don Miguel. *The Four Agreements: A Practical Guide to Personal Freedom*. San Rafael, CA: Amber-Allen Publishing, 2001.

Singer, Michael A. The Untethered Soul: The Journey Beyond Yourself. Oakland, CA: New Harbinger Publications, Inc, 2007.

van der Kolk, Bessel. *The Body Keeps the Score: Brain, Mind, and Body in the Healing of Trauma*. New York: Viking, 2014.

Welteroth, Elaine. *More Than Enough: Claiming Space for Who You Are (No Matter What They Say)*. New York: Viking, 2019.

WEBSITES

Therapy for Black Girls (website and podcast) TherapyforBlackGirls.com

References

AZquotes. Tracee Ellis Ross quote. azquotes.com/quote/1088836.

Christine Horn: Taking Hollywood by Storm. christinehorn.com/#:~:text=-Known%20to%20many%20as%20%E2%80%9CThe,To%20Becoming%20A%20Booking%20Magnet.%E2%80%9D.

Clemens, Danny. "Oprah Winfrey: 'Speaking Your Truth Is the Most Powerful Tool We All Have.'" ABC7 Eyewitness News. Arts & Entertainment. January 6, 2018. abc7.com/oprah-winfrey-cecil-b-demille-award-golden-globes-globe-awards/2879380/.

GoodReads. "Alice Walker Quotable Quote." goodreads.com/quotes/925242-don-t-wait-around-for-other-people-to-be-happy-for.

GoodReads. "Audre Lorde Quotable Quote." goodreads.com/quotes/437563-caring-for-myself-is-not-self-indulgence-it-is-self-preservation-and.

GoodReads. "Janet Autherine Quotable Quote." goodreads.com/quotes/10359579-when-you-understand-your-inner-self-your-passions-motivations.

GoodReads. "Lupita Nyong'o Quotable Quote." goodreads.com/quotes/1093806-you-can-t-eat-beauty-it-doesn-t-feed-you-beauty-was-not.

GoodReads. "Maya Angelou Quotable Quote." goodreads.com/quotes/11877-my-mission-in-life-is-not-merely-to-survive-but.

GoodReads. "Tony Morrison Quotable Quote." goodreads.com/quotes/18179-freeing-yourself-was-one-thing-claiming-ownership-of-that-freed.

Lawler, Kelly. "Ava DuVernay: 'Follow the White Guys.'" *USA Today*. People. July 20, 2015. usatoday.com/story/life/people/2015/07/20/ ava-duvernay-blogher-conference-follow--white-guys-Black-panther /30406529/.

Pittman, Jeremy. "10 Quotes to Inspire You to Never Settle in Life." Never Settle Foundation. September 1, 2020. neversettle.org/10-quote s-inspire-you-never-settle-life.

Quotes of Famous People. Kerry Washington quote. Last modified May 7, 2019. quotepark.com/quotes/1836849-kerry-washington-i-realized-that-i-dont -have-to-be-perfect-all-i.

Rodulfo, Kristina. "21 of Viola Davis's Most Inspiring Quotes." *Elle*. January 6, 2017. elle.com/culture/celebrities/a33069/viola-davis-inspiring-quotes.

ACKNOWLEDGMENTS

To all the Black women holding this book, I see you, I walk with you, and I root for your highest good always. My love for you, for us, runs deep.

Thank you to all the incredible Black women in my life, past and present, who have continuously poured into me. You've believed in me, affirmed me, prayed for me, and championed me fiercely throughout my life. I am eternally grateful for all that you are and all that you do. Thank you.

ABOUT THE AUTHOR

Sharron Lynn is an actor, author, Broadway performer, entrepreneur, and all-around wellness enthusiast. In 2017, she traveled to Rishikesh, India, to deepen her yoga knowledge and practice and complete her 200-hour yoga teacher training. She's also a certified mindfulness instructor and Reiki practitioner. With a passionate mission to spread the beauty and magic of yoga, meditation, and mindful living far and wide, Sharron founded Breathe Flow Be, a wellness community of self-lovers. Much of what she shares has been inspired by her own struggles and personal journey as well as the practices that help her maintain a life of love and joy. When she's not on a set or on stage, she's likely on a mat in her practice or working to share tools for well-being across various communities. Find her on Instagram and most other social media platforms at @iamsharronlynn.

CPSIA information can be obtained
at www.ICGtesting.com
Printed in the USA
LVHW070401241022
731392LV00017B/1054